YEARS 2 & 3

TIME

Do you need to know the basics of time? Let's learn about them together.

Parents and carers are encouraged to read the explanation and practice sections with their child.

Ann Baker

Illustrated by
Janice Bowles

About this book

Each unit in this book begins with a brief **explanation** of a concept or a strategy. You are encouraged to read this explanation with your child and, where appropriate, to use everyday materials and examples to give meaning to the concepts.

We practise is a worked example for you and your child to discuss together, paying particular attention to the thinking processes required to understand the concept or apply the strategy.

You practise gives your child the opportunity to practise the concept or strategy. It also indicates how well your child understands the new material and often includes problem-solving questions to ensure that your child has mastered the concept or strategy.

If further support is required, you and your child's teacher can devise a plan to ensure that all the basic concepts are fully understood and consolidated.

The **Tests** at the end of the book are provided to check that the concepts are fully understood. Test 1 can be done after units 1–10 are completed and Test 2 when the book is finished.

Meet 'BOB' – Back Of the Book

At the end of each unit, BOB reminds your child to go to the Answers section at the back of the book.

Mathematical Content

This book has been designed to cover the concepts of time that your child will encounter in **Year 2** and **Year 3**. The units provide a comprehensive coverage of the following Key Topics from the **Australian Curriculum: Mathematics**.

Australian Curriculum : Mathematics

YEAR 2

Tell time to the quarter hour, using the language of 'past' and 'to' (ACMMG039)

Name and order months and seasons (ACMMG040)

Use a calendar to identify the date and determine the number of days in each month (ACMMG041)

YEAR 3

Tell time to the minute and investigate the relationship between units of time (ACMMG062)

Contents & Checklist

WRITING and TALKING ABOUT TIME

The language of time presents difficulties for students. Words such as *before, later, tomorrow, yesterday, last week* and *next week* do not initially have a clear meaning to them, but you can help with this by using such terms with care and with frequency.

For instance you might ask, *Do you remember where we went the day before yesterday?* You can then help your child mentally backtrack to the event.

Talk to your child about *midday* and *midnight* and that there are twelve hours between each, and 24 hours in a day. Explain how the hour hand goes around the clock twice in every day.

Duration of time periods is an essential part of learning about time.

Do not give mixed messages, for instance saying 'in a minute' when you mean 15 minutes.

Similarly, when your child asks how long to a particular time, don't just tell them but point them to a clock. Help them read the present time and work out how long to go until the specified time.

Understanding the difference between a past the hour time and a to the hour time presents many difficulties in the early stages of learning to tell the time.

When reading times with your child, take care to draw attention to the position of the hour hand. When it is halfway between two numbers explain that the clock face is showing a 'past the hour' time. When it is more than halfway between two numbers, explain that it is showing a 'to the hour' time.

GAME CARD IDEAS

Cut out the game cards – they will last longer if they are laminated. Here are some games for you to try.

Memory

Use only the o'clock game cards initially and set them out face down in an array. Take turns to turn over two cards. If they make a matching time pair they are set to one side and that player takes another turn. If not, they are turned over and play passes to the next player. The player who has made most pairs is the winner of that game.

At appropriate times the other cards – half hour, quarter to and quarter past – can be included in the game.

Sequences

Introduce this game with the o' clock and half past cards only. Players are dealt 4 cards. On their turn a player can discard a card and take another from the pack. The goal of the game is to be the first player to make a time sequence, for example, 11:30, 12:00. 12:30. As appropriate, introduce the other cards to the game but deal 6 cards and make sequences with 5 times in sequence.

Strategic Sequences

This game is played like 'Sequences' except that the deck of cards is set out with the cards face up, not face down, and the discarded cards are also face up.

This means that players can plan to block their opponents or to change sequence if they can see it is necessary.

NOTE: Games are meant to be fun and provide practice without stress. It is recommended that you stop playing while you are still having fun and then your child will want to play again another time.

UNIT 1

THE HOUR HAND

This is a clock face.

The numbers on the clock face name the hours.

There are **two hands** on a clock face – the **hour hand** and the **minute hand**.

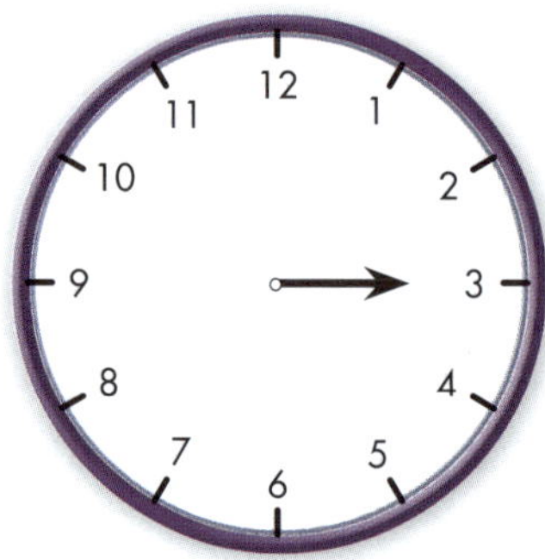

This clock face only shows the **short hand,** which is called the **hour hand**.

The hour hand is pointing at the 3. The clock face is showing **3 o'clock**.

We practise

Where will the hour hand be pointing when it is 4 o'clock?

What o'clock time is this clock face showing?

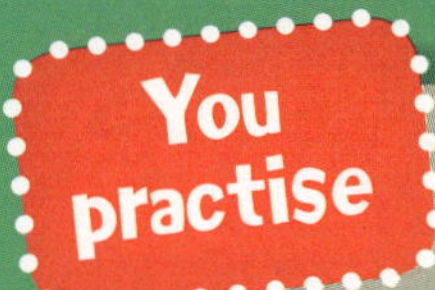

Show where the hour hand will be pointing at these times.

9 o'clock

11 o'clock

Remember that the **hour** hand is the **short hand**.

2 o'clock

12 o'clock

What o'clock times are these clock faces showing?

______ o'clock

______ o'clock

______ o'clock

______ o'clock

______ o'clock

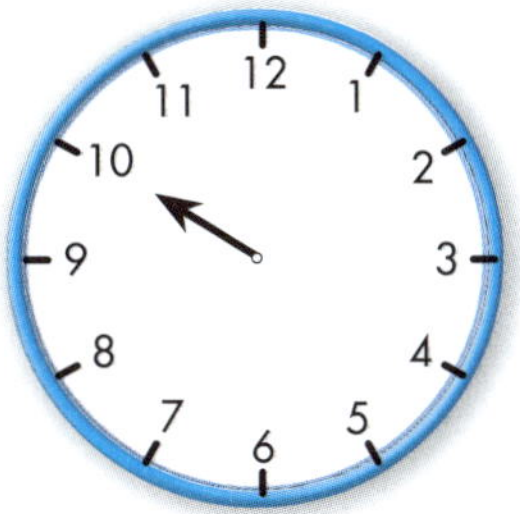

______ o'clock

TELLING the O'CLOCK TIMES

You know that the short hand points to the hours.
The long hand is called the minute hand.

When it is an o'clock time the minute hand points straight up at the twelve.

On this clock face, the hour hand is pointing to the 3 and the minute hand is pointing straight up to the 12.
This clock face is showing **3 o'clock**.

The hour hand on this clock face is pointing at the 4 so it is **4 o'clock**.

Remember to look where the hour hand is pointing to find out the hour time.

We practise

What time is this clock face showing?

The clock face is showing 5 o'clock.

Draw the hands on this clock face to show 7 o'clock.

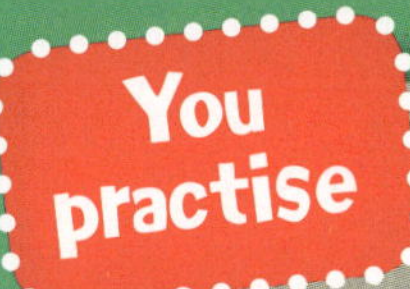

What times are these clock faces showing?

_____ o'clock

_____ o'clock

_____ o'clock

_____ o'clock

Draw the hands on these clock faces to show the o'clock times.

Remember to make the **hour** hand the **short** hand and the **minute** hand the **long** hand.

5 8 o'clock

6 2 o'clock

7 7 o'clock

8 11 o'clock

9 1 o'clock

10 12 o'clock

BOB time!

DIGITAL CLOCKS

A digital clock looks like this.

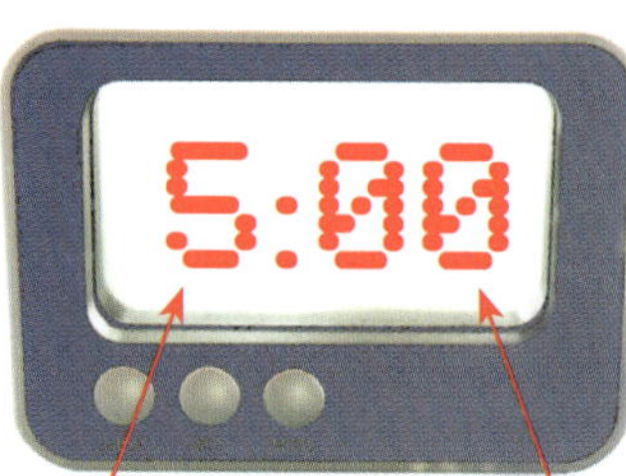

This number shows the **hour.**

These numbers show the **minutes.**

The time on the digital clock is **5 o'clock.**
The two zeros tell us that it is an o'clock time.

You can show time:

in words — seven o'clock

on a digital clock — 7:00

on an analogue clock.

We practise

Show 8 o'clock on this digital clock.

8:00

Write the time shown on this analogue clock in words and on the digital clock.

3:00

The time is three o'clock.

You practise

Show the times on the digital clocks.

1. 5 o'clock   __ __ : __ __

2. 9 o'clock   __ __ : __ __

3. 11 o'clock

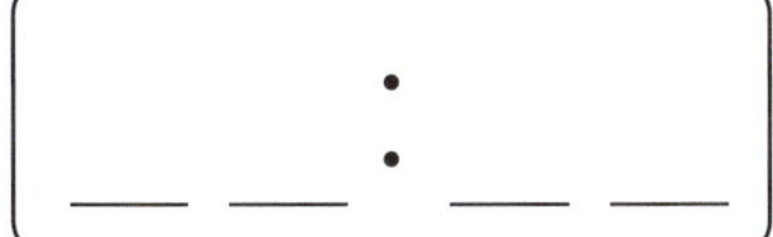

4. 3 o'clock

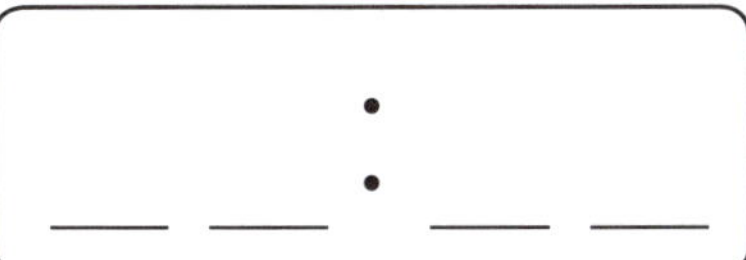

Remember the zero minutes when you show an o'clock time.

You practise

Write the time shown on each analogue clock in words and on the digital clock.

5.

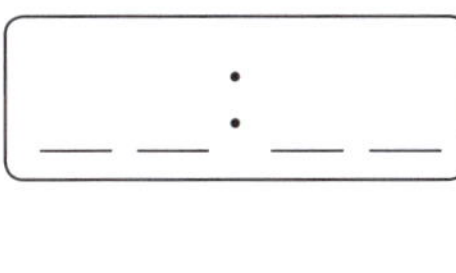

________ o'clock

6.

__ __ : __ __

________ o'clock

BOB time!

7.

__ __ : __ __

________ o'clock

8.

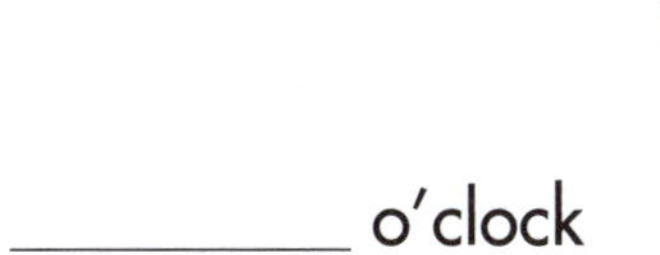

________ o'clock

9.

__ __ : __ __

________ o'clock

10.

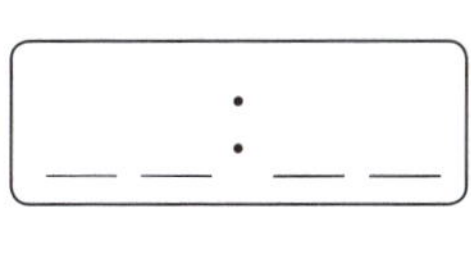

________ o'clock

SEQUENCING TIMES

There are 24 hours in a day.

The hour hand on the clock goes all the way around from 12 o'clock midnight to 12 o'clock midday and then round again to 12 o'clock midnight.

We use timetables to help us organise the 24 hours in our day.

This is Jai's timetable for Saturday.

SATURDAY	
7 o'clock	breakfast
8 o'clock	help Dad with the car wash
10 o'clock	junior footy training
12 o'clock	lunch with Gran
3 o'clock	movies with a friend
6 o'clock	family dinner
8 o'clock	favourite TV show

Remember that 1 o'clock comes next after 12 o'clock.

We practise

Write the digital time for each event in the correct order and then draw a line to match each event with the digital time.

walk the dog – 10 o'clock

have lunch – 1 o'clock

have breakfast – 7 o'clock

7:00

10:00

1:00

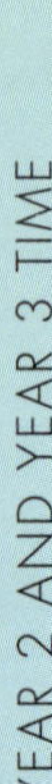

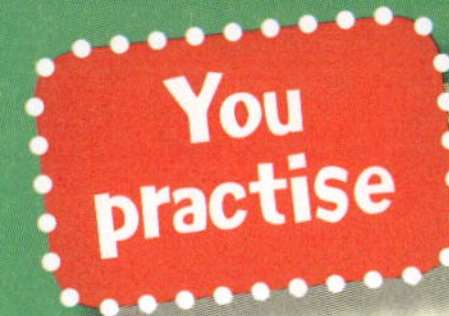

Write the digital time for each event in the correct order and then draw a line to match each event with the digital time.

Look for the first and last thing in the day to help you get started.

Event	Digital time
Bedtime – 9 o'clock	__ __ : __ __
Breakfast – 8 o'clock	__ __ : __ __
Lunch time – 12 o'clock	__ __ : __ __
Dinner time – 7 o'clock	__ __ : __ __
Get out of bed – 7 o'clock	__ __ : __ __
Watch TV – 8 o'clock	__ __ : __ __
Karate – 5 o'clock	__ __ : __ __
Haircut – 10 o'clock	__ __ : __ __
Meet friend for afternoon walk – 2 o'clock	__ __ : __ __
Afternoon snack with Mum – 4 o'clock	__ __ : __ __

BOB time!

UNIT 5 TELLING the HALF PAST the HOUR TIMES

When the minute hand is pointing to the 12 it is an o'clock time.

This clock shows **3 o'clock**.

When the minute hand is pointing down at the 6 it is a half past the hour time.

This clock shows **half past three** and the clock face has been coloured to show that there are two half hours in an hour.

Notice how far the hour hand has moved. It is now halfway between the 3 and the 4. Whenever the time is half past the hour the hour hand is halfway between two numbers on the clock face.

We practise

What time is this clock face showing?

Half past one

Draw the hour and minute hands on this clock face to show half past seven.

You practise

What times are these clock faces showing?

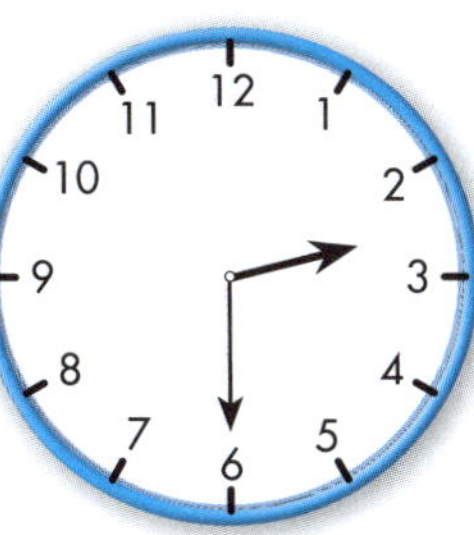

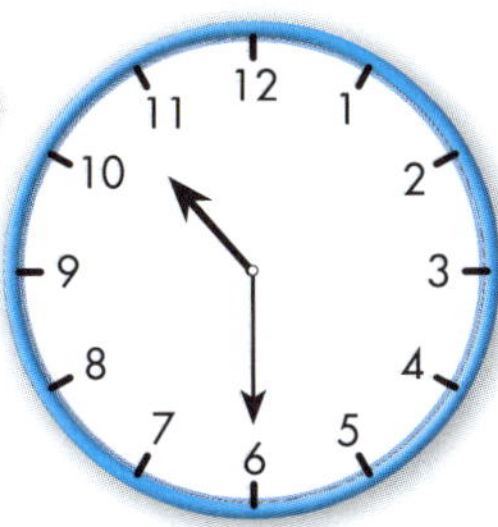

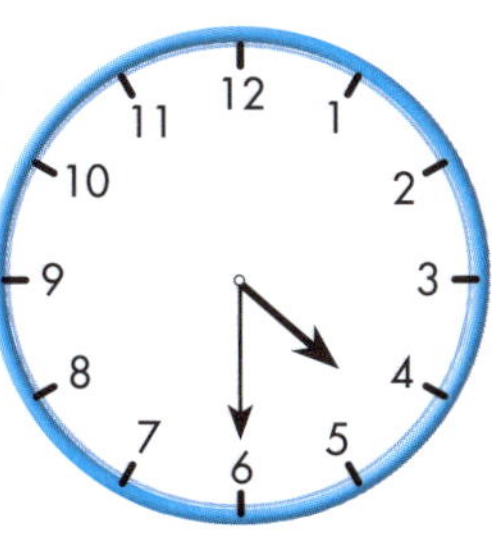

You practise

Draw the minute and hour hands on each clock face to show the half past time.

Half past eight

Half past eleven

Half past three

Half past six

Think about where the hour hand should be pointing when it is a half past the hour time.

Half past one

Half past nine

BOB time!

HALF HOUR TIMES on DIGITAL CLOCKS

When it is an o'clock time there are no minutes past the hour.

There are two zeroes in the minutes section of a digital clock. For example, this clock is showing 5 o'clock.

There are 60 minutes in an hour.

When it is half past the hour, half of 60 is 30, so the digital clock looks like this.

The time on this digital clock is read as five thirty which means the same as half past five.

We practise

Write the time showing on this digital clock as a half past time.

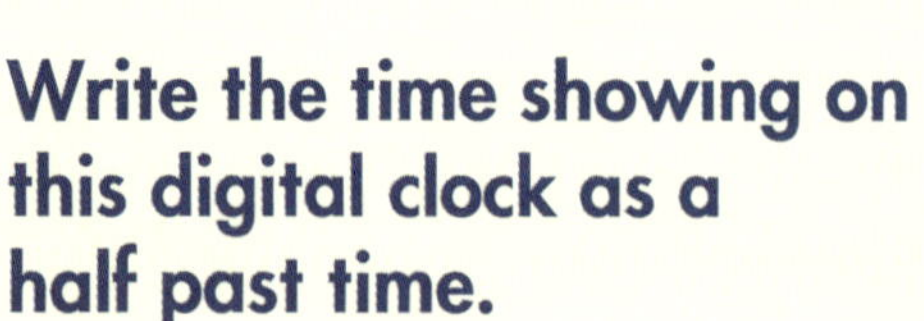

Half past ten

Show half past six on this digital clock.

6:30

You practise

Write the times showing on these digital clocks as a half past time.

9:30

____

7:30

____

Remember that 30 in the minutes section is the same as **half past**.

4:30

____

11:30

____

You practise

Show these half past times on the digital clocks.

Half past three

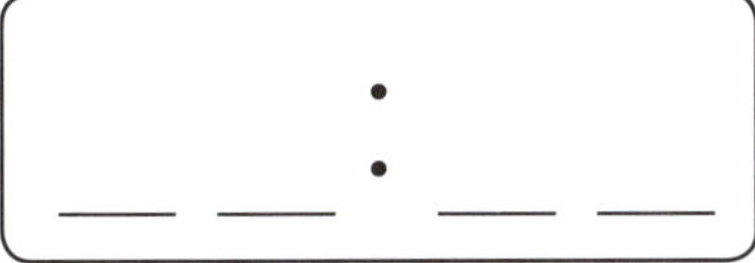

Half past eight

Half past eleven

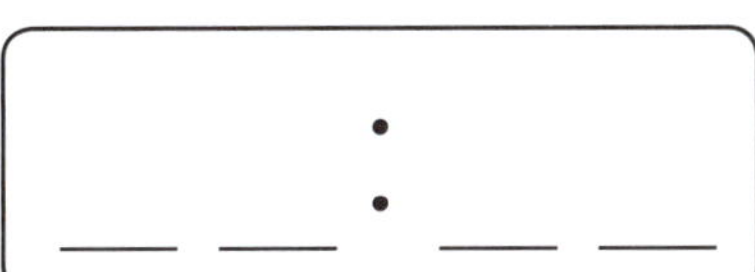

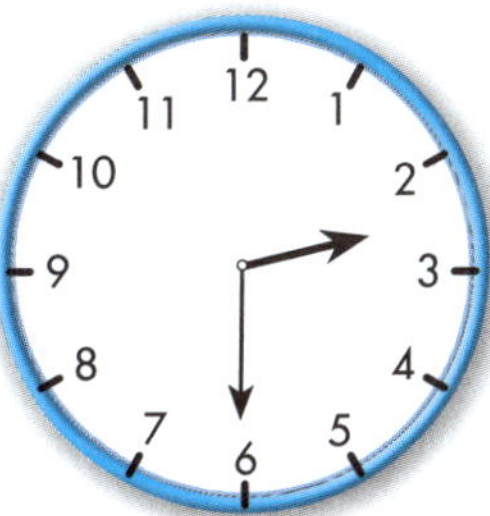

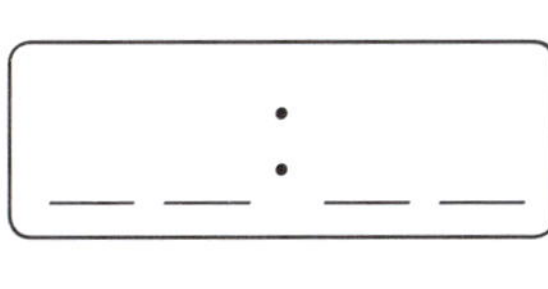

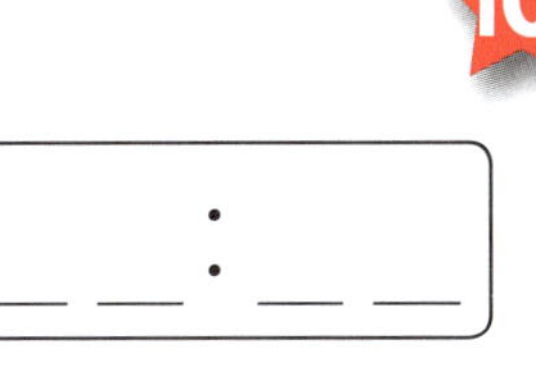

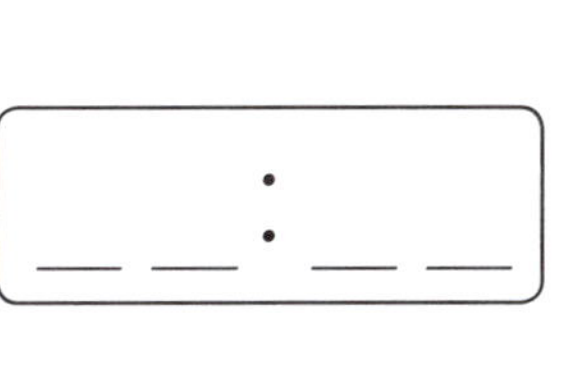

BOB time!

DAYS OF THE WEEK

There are **seven days** in a week.

Monday

Tuesday

Wednesday

Thursday

Friday

These are the **weekdays** when you go to school.

Saturday

Sunday

These are the **weekend** days when you stay home.

Sunday is followed by Monday and the weekdays begin again.

Tomorrow is the word that means **the next day**.

Yesterday is the word that means **the day before**.

Two weeks together makes 14 days and is called a **fortnight**.

We practise

Which day is the day before Wednesday?

Tuesday

If today were Saturday what day would it be tomorrow?

Sunday

You practise Fill in the days.

Use the list of days opposite if you need to.

1 Which day comes after Thursday? ____________

2 Which day comes before Thursday? ____________

3 Which weekend day is the day before you go to school? ____________

4 Which day comes between Wednesday and Friday? ____________

5 Which days are at the weekend?

____________ and ____________

6 If today is Saturday, what day will it be tomorrow? ____________

7 If today is Saturday, what day was it yesterday? ____________

8 If today is the last day of the school week, what day will it be tomorrow? ____________

9 If yesterday was Monday, what day will it be tomorrow? ____________

10 If tomorrow is Thursday, what day was it yesterday? ____________

BOB time!

QUARTER PAST TIMES on ANALOGUE CLOCKS

At **quarter past** the hour the minute hand has travelled a quarter of the way around the analogue clock face.

This clock shows **quarter past 1**.
At quarter past the hour the hour hand has moved a little way past the hour.

Can you see that the hour hand has travelled just past the 1? It is only a **quarter** of the way between 1 and 2.

We practise

What time does this clock face show?

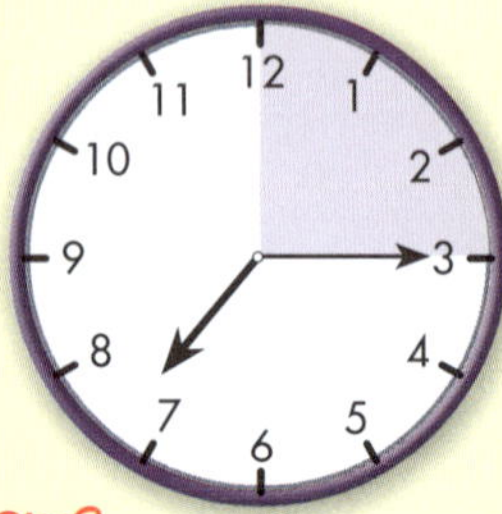

This clock shows quarter past seven.

Draw the hands on this clock face to show quarter past six.

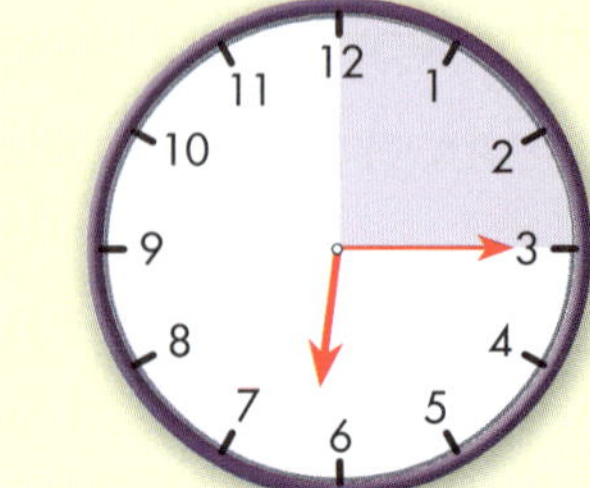

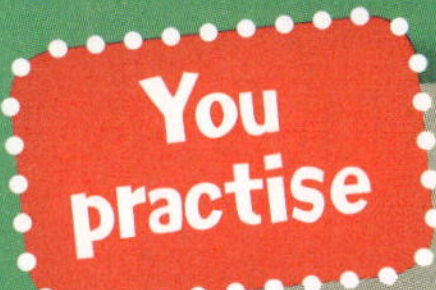

What time does each analogue clock face show?

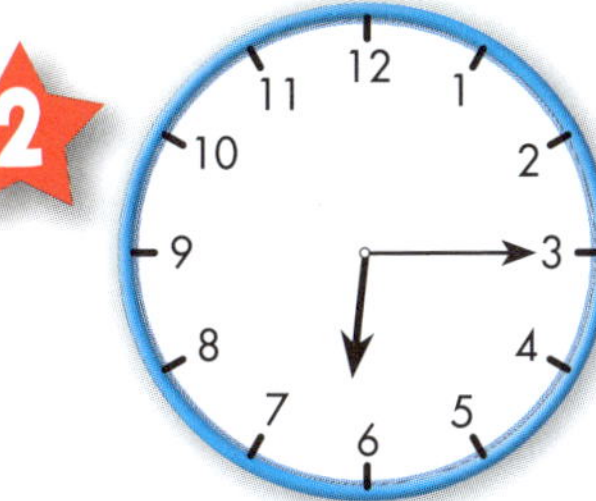

You practise

Draw the hour and minute hands on each analogue clock face to show the quarter past time.

Quarter past four

Quarter past eleven

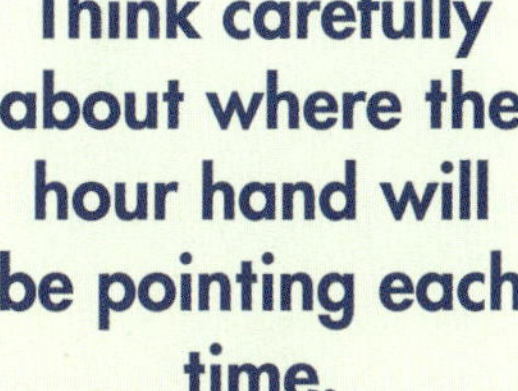

Quarter past twelve

Quarter past eight

Quarter past five

Quarter past three

BOB time!

QUARTER PAST TIMES on a DIGITAL CLOCK

There are 60 minutes in an hour, so there are 30 minutes in half an hour.

This shows on the digital clock as 30 in the minutes section.
For example, half past 10 shows on a digital clock as:

Half of 30 is 15, so there are 15 minutes in a quarter of an hour.

This shows on the digital clock as 15 in the minutes section.
For example, quarter past 10 shows on a digital clock as:

We read this as **ten fifteen**.

We practise

What quarter past time does this clock show?

8:15

This clock shows quarter past 8.

Show quarter past six on this digital clock.

6:15

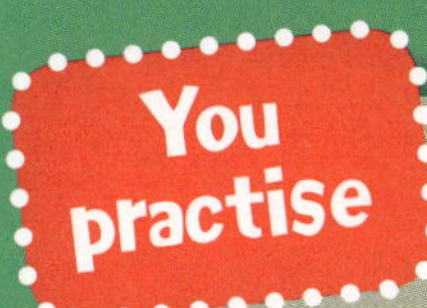

What quarter past time does each digital clock show?

1:15

4:15

6:15

5:15

Notice the colon is between the hours and the minutes.

Show each quarter past time on the digital clock.

Quarter past nine

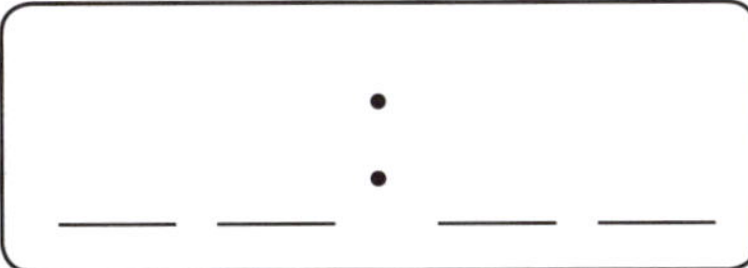

Quarter past two

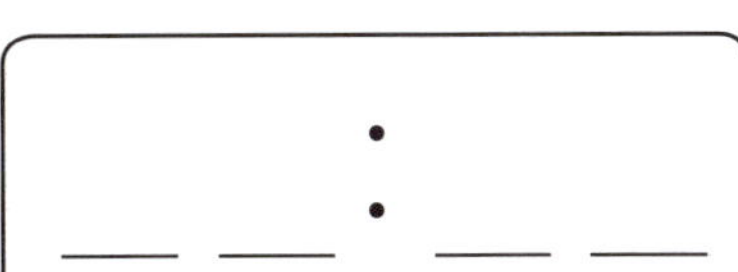

Quarter past seven

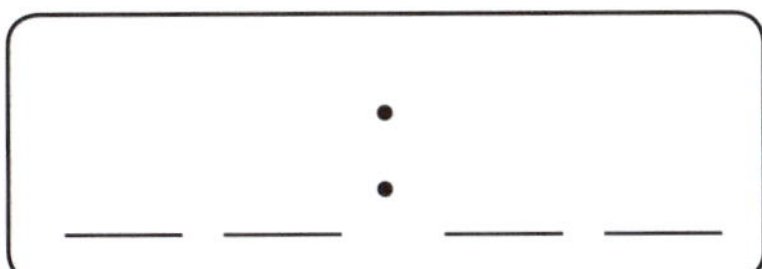

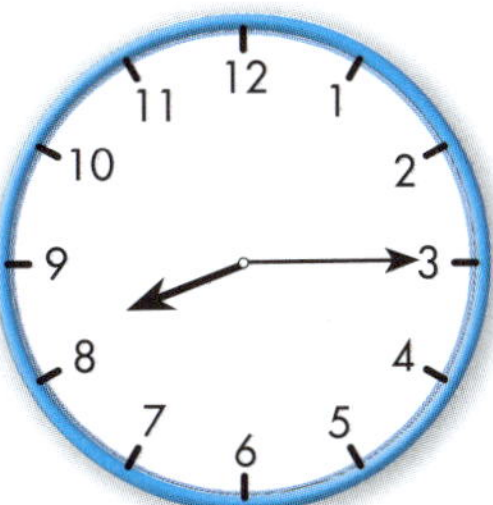

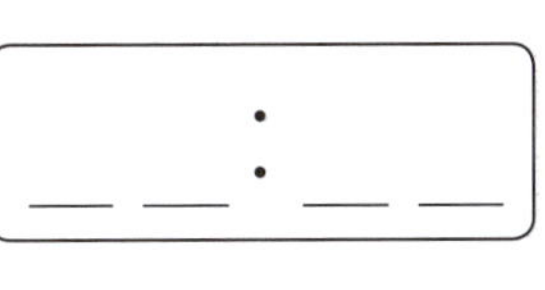

BOB time!

PROBLEM SOLVING with TIME

A Time Problem

Jake had dinner at

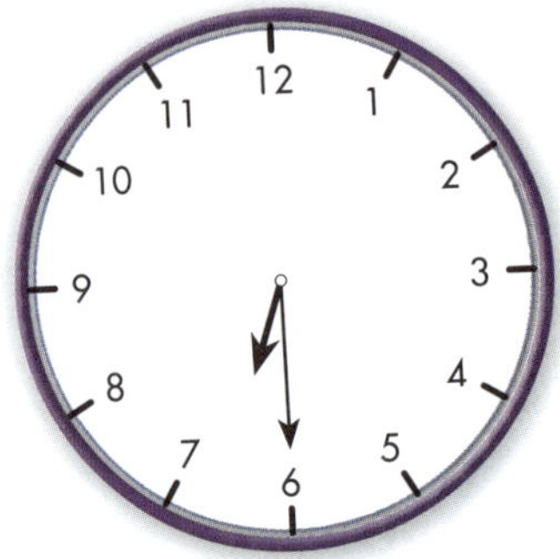

Clare said she had dinner half an hour later than Jake.
Max said he had dinner half an hour earlier than Jake.
What time did Clare and Max have dinner?

Notice how the important information is highlighted in blue.

Notice how what has to be found out is highlighted in pink.

This helps you to find all the important information in this problem.

Writing the times in order can help solve this problem.

DINNER TIME

Max	Jake	Clare
6:00	6:30	7:00

Answer: Clare had dinner at 7:00 and Max had dinner at 6:00.

We practise

Highlight the important information in this problem, then draw a time diagram to find the answer.

Clare went to see Ice Age 3. The movie began at 4 o'clock. It lasted for two hours. What time did the movie finish?

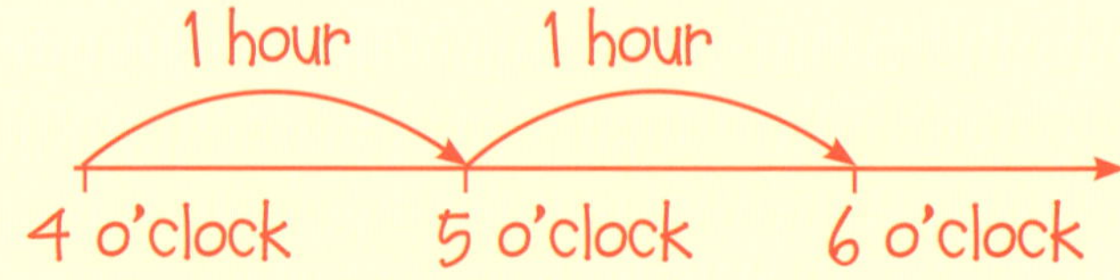

Answer: The movie finished at 6 o'clock.

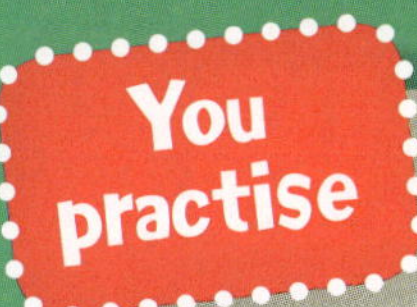

Highlight the important information in these problems, then answer them.

1 Clare set her digital clock to a quarter past 6.
What did her clock look like? __ __ : __ __

On Friday Jake said he was going to a party tomorrow.
What day was the party? ________________

On Wednesday Clare said it was three days until her birthday. What day was her birthday? ________________

Clare said she went to the dentist the day before yesterday.
It is Friday now. Which day did Clare go to the dentist? ________________

'What time will it be two hours after midday?'
Clare asked Jake. ________________

'Cricket starts at half past three,' Jake told his younger brother.
'What will the clocks look like at half past three?' his brother wanted to know.

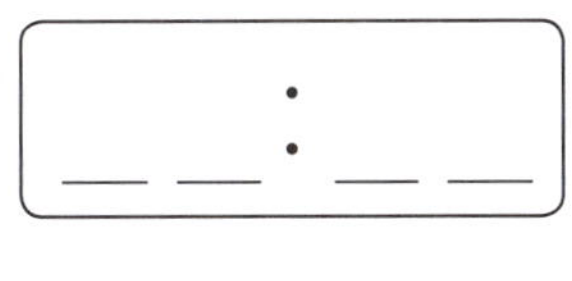

Jake looked at his watch.
Then he said that he needed two more hours to finish his project.
What time will the project be finished? ________________

Max likes to play with the clocks in his house. He set them all to a quarter past five.
What did the digital and the analogue clocks look like at that time?

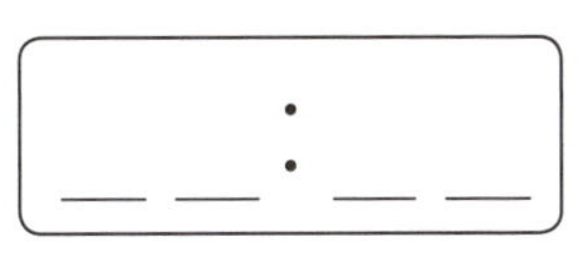

BOB time!

UNIT 11 MONTHS AND SEASONS

1	January
2	February
3	March
4	April
5	May
6	June
7	July
8	August
9	September
10	October
11	November
12	December

Each year there are **four seasons**: spring, summer, autumn and winter.

This diagram shows how the months fit into each season.

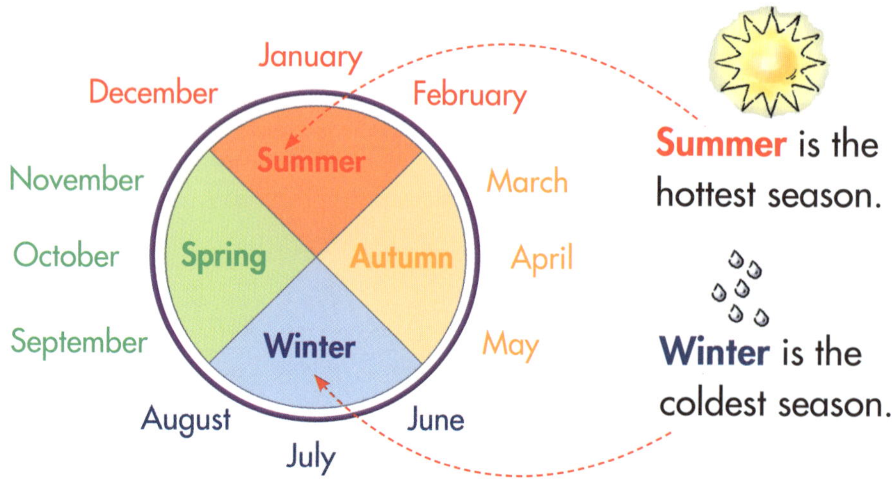

We practise

Which month comes after August?

September comes after August.

Which is the first month of autumn?

March is the first month of autumn.

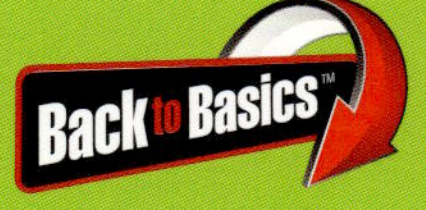

TIME

YEARS 2 and 3

TIME

YEARS 2 and 3

TIME

YEARS 2 and 3

TIME

YEARS 2 and 3

TIME

YEARS 2 and 3

TIME

YEARS 2 and 3

TIME

YEARS 2 and 3

TIME

YEARS 2 and 3

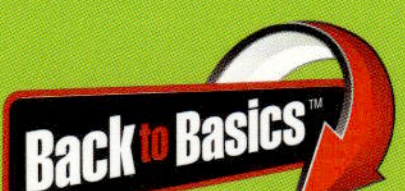

TIME

YEARS 2 and 3

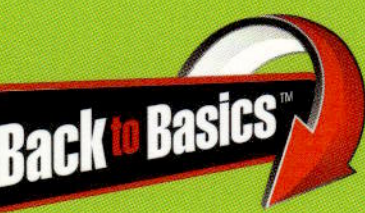

TIME

YEARS 2 and 3

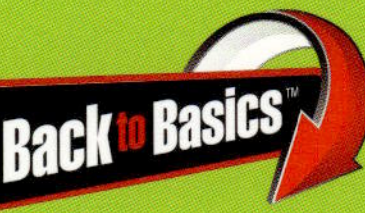

TIME

YEARS 2 and 3

TIME

YEARS 2 and 3

TIME

YEARS 2 and 3

Back to Basics

TIME

YEARS 2 and 3

TIME

YEARS 2 and 3

TIME

YEARS 2 and 3

11:00

11:30

12:00

12:30

1:00

1:30

2:00

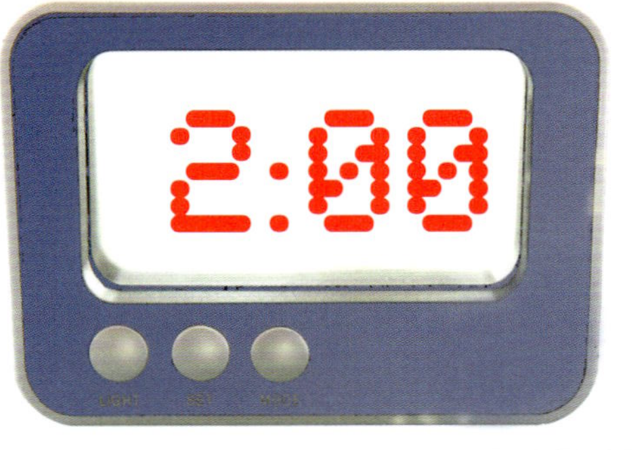

2:30

11:15		**11:45**	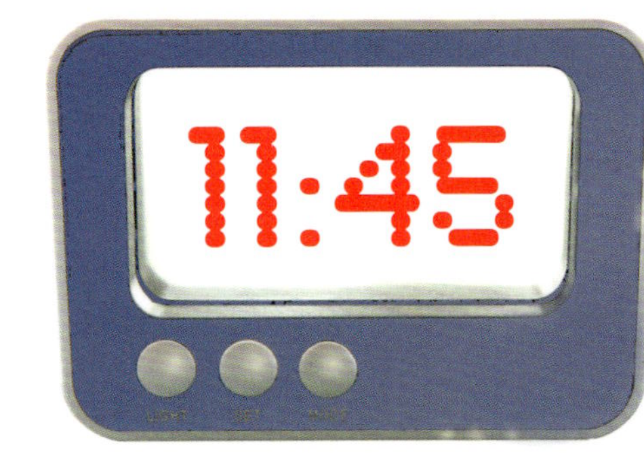
12:15		**12:45**	
1:15		**1:45**	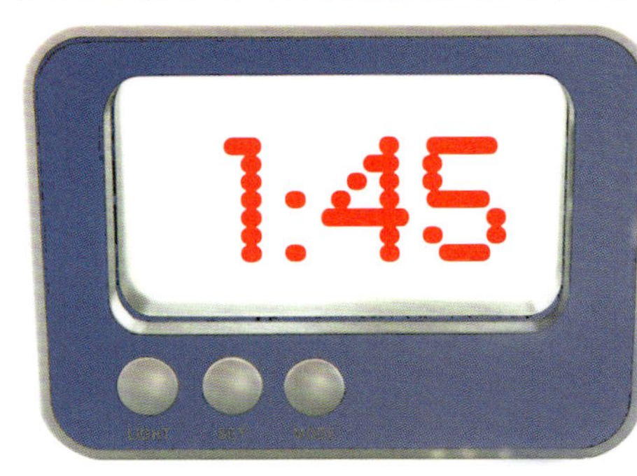
2:15	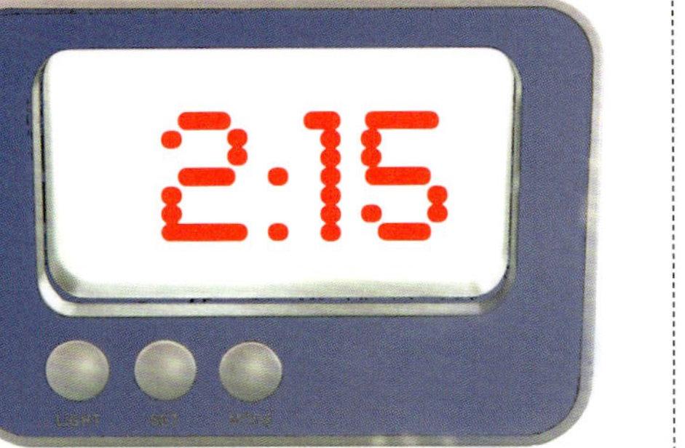	**2:45**	

TIME

YEARS 2 and 3

TIME

YEARS 2 and 3

TIME

YEARS 2 and 3

TIME

YEARS 2 and 3

TIME

YEARS 2 and 3

TIME

YEARS 2 and 3

TIME

YEARS 2 and 3

Back to Basics

TIME

YEARS 2 and 3

Back to Basics

TIME

YEARS 2 and 3

Back to Basics

TIME

YEARS 2 and 3

TIME

YEARS 2 and 3

TIME

YEARS 2 and 3

TIME

YEARS 2 and 3

TIME

YEARS 2 and 3

TIME

YEARS 2 and 3

Back to Basics

TIME

YEARS 2 and 3

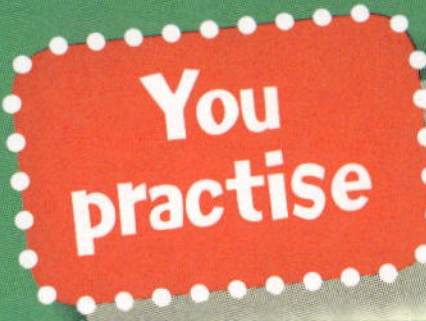

Write the months.

Use the list of months opposite if you need to.

1. Which month comes before December? ______________________
2. Which month comes after June? ______________________
3. Which month comes between February and April? ______________________
4. Which is the first month of the year? ______________________
5. Which month comes after December? ______________________
6. Which is the first month of winter? ______________________
7. Which season comes before spring? ______________________
8. Which season comes after spring? ______________________
9. Which season is the coldest? ______________________
10. Which season is the warmest? ______________________

BOB time!

CALENDARS

This is a page from a calendar for October 2013.
The weekdays are shaded green and the weekend is shaded blue.

OCTOBER 2013						
Sunday	Monday	Tuesday	Wednesday	Thursday	Friday	Saturday
		1	2	3	4	5
6	7	8	9	10	11	12
13	14 Clare to dentist	15	16	17	18	19
20 Aunt Vera to Grandma's	21	22	23	24	25 David's birthday	26
27	28	29	30	31		

The calendar shows that:

Clare is going to the dentist on **Monday, 14th of October**.
Look down the Mondays until you come to the 14 to find 14th October.

Jake is going to David's birthday party on **Friday, 25th October**.
Find the Fridays then run your finger down the page to find Friday 25th.

Use the calendar to find what day of the week 24th October is.

Thursday

We practise

Use the calendar to find out on what day and date Aunt Vera goes to visit Grandma.

Sunday, 20th October

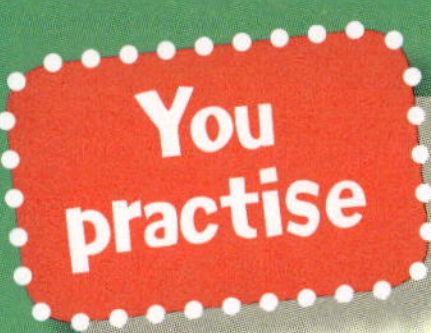

Use this calendar for December 2013 to answer the questions below.

DECEMBER 2013						
Sun	Mon	Tues	Wed	Thur	Fri	Sat
1	2	3 Choir	4	5	6	7
8	9	10 Choir	11	12	13 End of term	14
15	16	17 Choir	18 Jake: Karate comp	19	20	21
22	23	24	25	26	27 Ann's birthday	28
29	30	31				

1. When does Clare go to a birthday party? ______________
2. What date is Jake's karate competition? ______________
3. Which day of the week does Mum go to choir? ______________
4. What is the date of the day after the last day of school? ______________
5. What month and year follow December 2013? ______________ ________
6. How many times does Mum go to choir in December? ______________
7. If Ann is 13 years old on her birthday, what year was she born? ______________
8. How many Sundays are there in December 2013? ______________
9. What is the date of the fourth Monday in December 2013? ______________
10. Pick any weekday in the second or third week of December and shade the dates around it in these colours. What pattern can you find by adding the numbers that have the same colour?

____

BOB time!

UNIT 13

QUARTER TO TIMES on ANALOGUE CLOCKS

There are 15 minutes in a quarter of an hour.

15 minutes is a quarter of the way around the clock face.

There are 30 minutes in half an hour.

30 minutes is half the way around the clock face.

There are 45 minutes in three quarters of an hour.

45 minutes is three quarters of the way around the clock face.

When the minute hand is three quarters of an hour past the o'clock, there is only one quarter of an hour to go until the next o'clock. This is why we say **quarter to** the hour rather than **three quarters past** the hour. For example, this clock shows the time as 45 minutes past five, which we say as **quarter to six**.

We practise

What quarter to time does this clock show?

Quarter to two

Show quarter to eight on this clock.

You practise — What quarter to time does each analogue clock show?

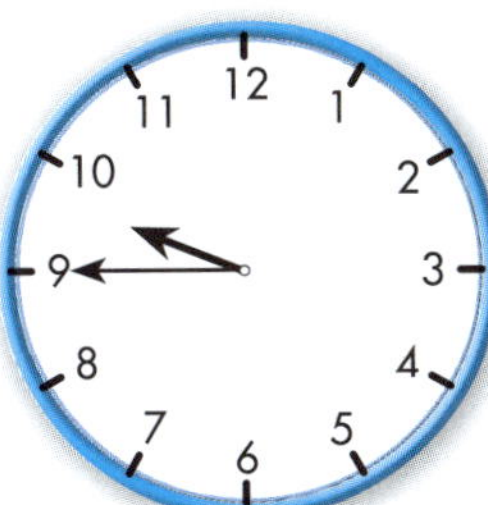

Quarter to __________

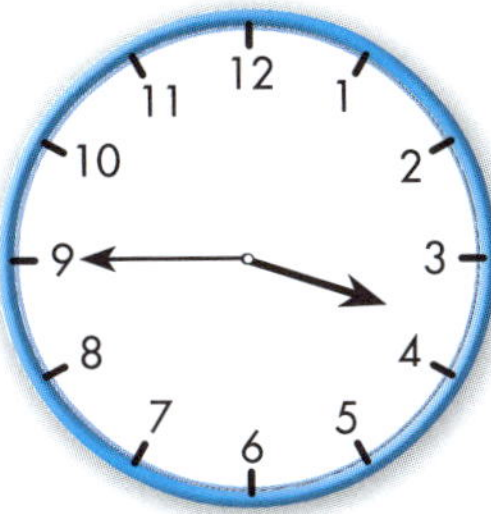

Quarter to __________

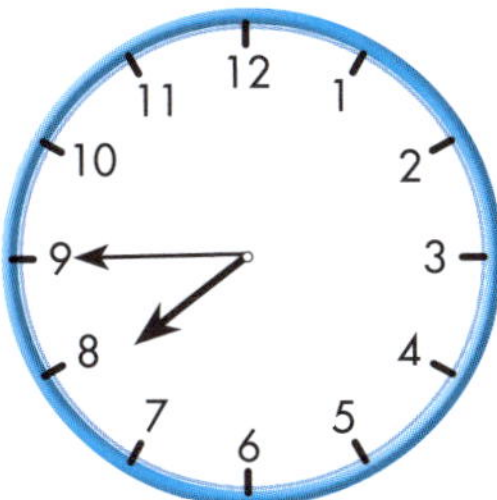

Quarter to __________

Quarter to __________

You practise — Show each quarter to time on the analogue clock.

5 Quarter to nine

Quarter to five

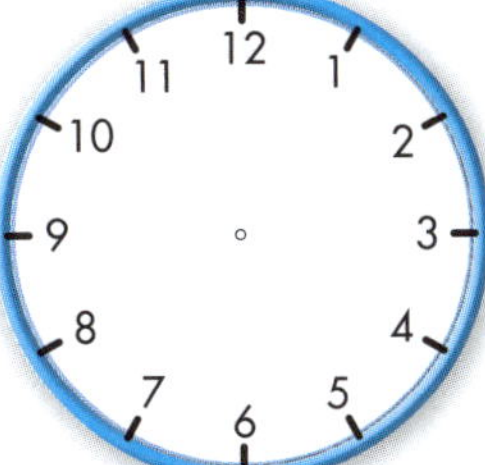

7 Quarter to twelve

Quarter to three

9 Quarter to seven

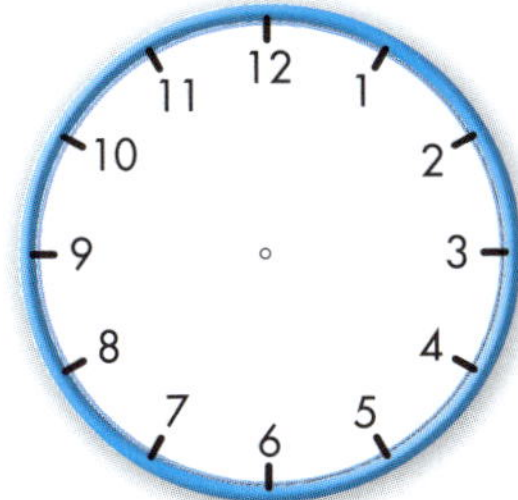

10 Quarter to one

Think carefully about where the hour hand is pointing.

BOB time!

QUARTER TO TIMES on DIGITAL CLOCKS

There are 15 minutes in a quarter of an hour.

Quarter past is shown by the number **15** in the minutes section of a digital clock.

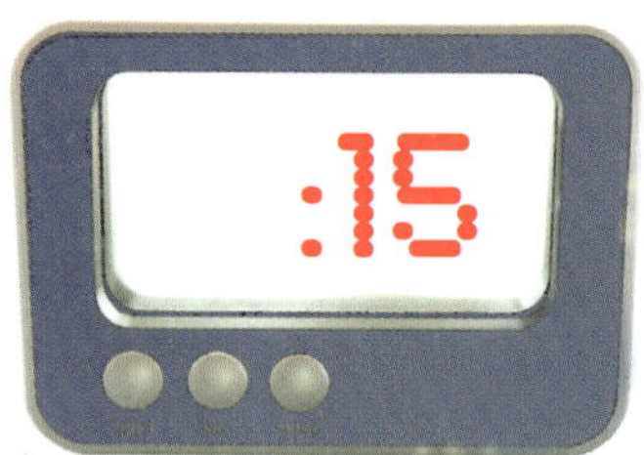

There are 45 minutes in three quarters of an hour.

Quarter to times are shown by the number **45** in the minutes section of a digital clock.

5:45

This clock face shows a quarter to 6, which is the same as 45 minutes past 5.

On a digital clock, we read this time as **five forty-five**.

Five forty-five and **quarter to six** are just two different ways of saying the same time.

We practise

What quarter to time does this digital clock show?

5:45

Quarter to six

Show quarter to eight on both of these clocks.

7:45

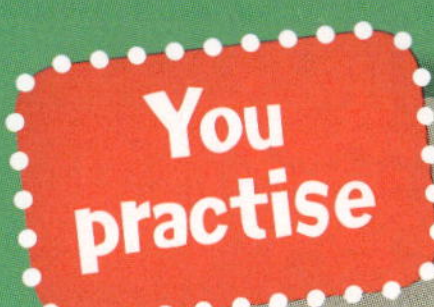

What quarter to time does each digital clock show?

1:45

Quarter to ___________

3:45

Quarter to ___________

Think carefully about which hour they show a quarter to.

10:45

Quarter to ___________

12:45

Quarter to ___________

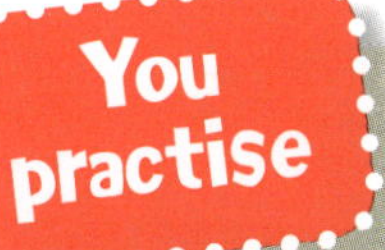

Show each quarter to time on the clock.

Quarter to 8

__ __ : __ __

Seven forty-five

__ __ : __ __

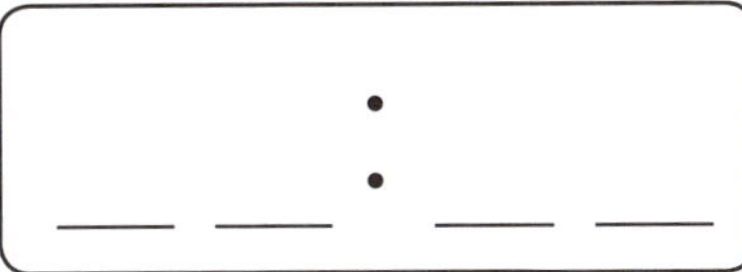

Quarter to 12

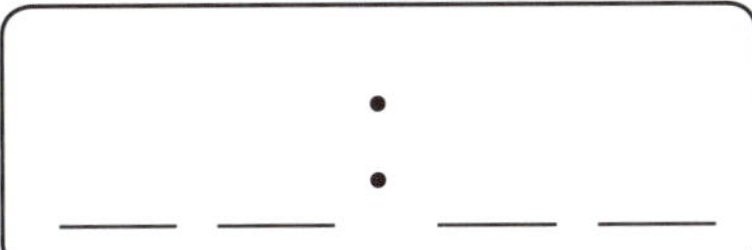

Twelve forty-five

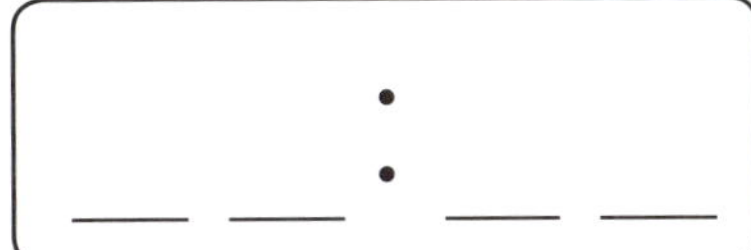

3:45

6:45

BOB time!

FIVE MINUTE INTERVALS on ANALOGUE CLOCKS

Around the edge of the clock face you can see large marks next to each number.

These marks show the hours for the hour hand but also show intervals of 5 minutes for the minute hand. You can count all around the clock face in 5s until you get back to the beginning. By then you will have counted to 60, the number of minutes in one hour.

This clock shows **twenty-five past three.**

It is a **past the hour** time because the hour hand has moved past 3 and the minute hand points to 5, showing that $5 \times 5 = 25$ minutes have passed since the o'clock.

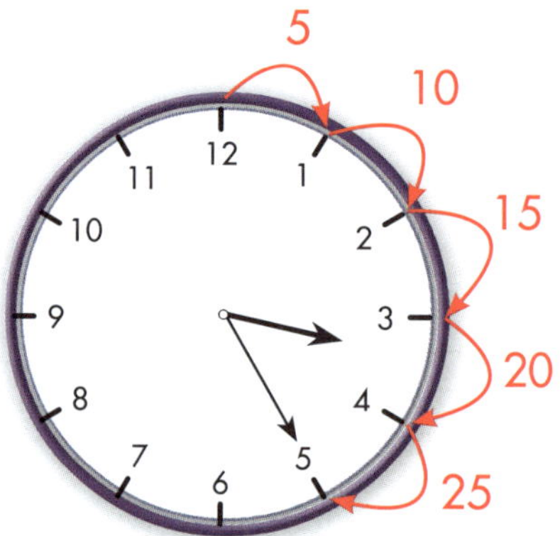

Count the minutes past the hour: 5, 10, 15, 20, 25.

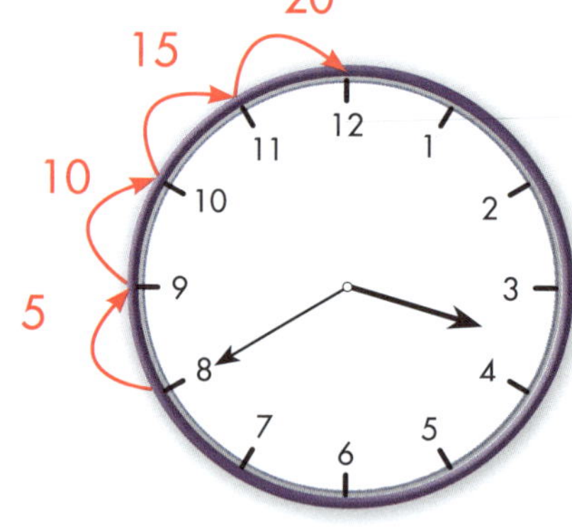

This clock shows **twenty to four.**

The hour hand is getting close to 4 and the minute hand is pointing to 8. If we count on in 5s to the o'clock, we are counting the minutes to the next hour.

We practise

Show twenty minutes past nine on this clock.

Show 10 minutes to 4 on this clock.

It is really important to think about where the hour hand is pointing each time.

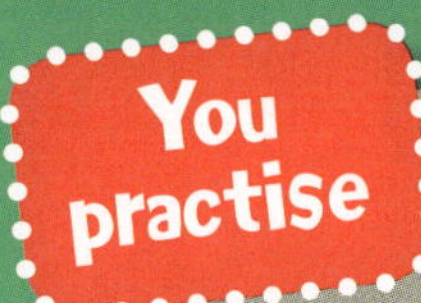

Show each 'past' time on the clock.

Twenty past six

5 minutes past 7

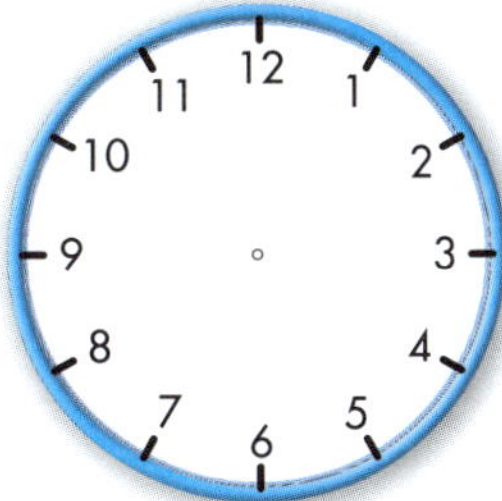

Remember to think about where the hour hand will be pointing each time.

Twenty-five past eight

15 minutes past 3

You practise

Show each 'to' time on the clock.

Twenty to six

15 minutes to 7

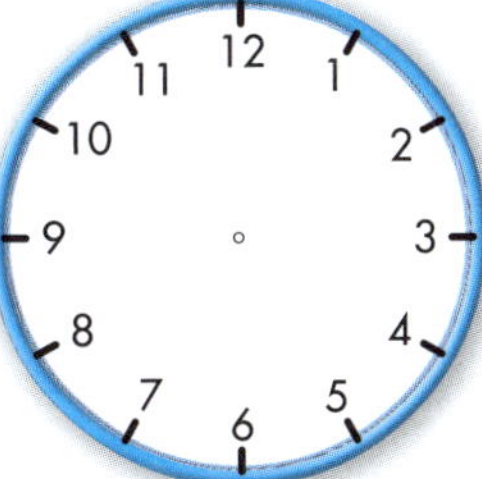

25 minutes to 11

15 minutes to 12

5 to 7

Twenty to twelve

FIVE MINUTE INTERVALS on DIGITAL CLOCKS

As you know, on a digital clock the hour comes first, followed by the minutes.

This time is read as **five twenty-five** and means twenty-five minutes past 5 o'clock.

Use the analogue clock face to help you work out how many minutes until the next o'clock time.

On a digital clock only the minutes past the hour are given. For example, the clock below shows fifty-five minutes past three o'clock.

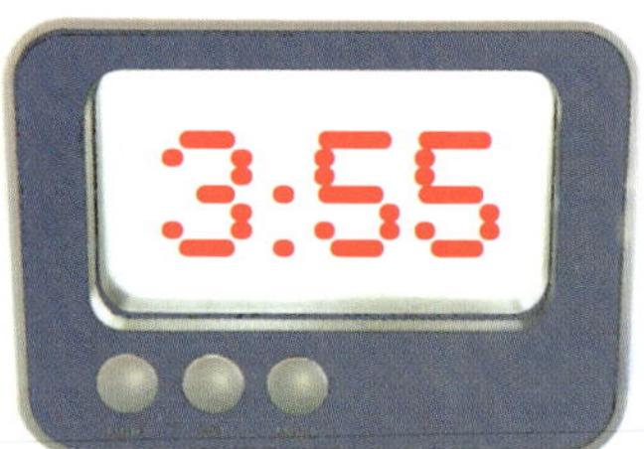

This time is read as **three fifty-five**, but you can also read it as a 'to the hour' time.

To work out how many minutes to the next o'clock, you subtract the number of minutes shown from 60. In this case there are 60 – 55 = 5 minutes. So the time can also be read as **five minutes to four**.

5 minutes to go

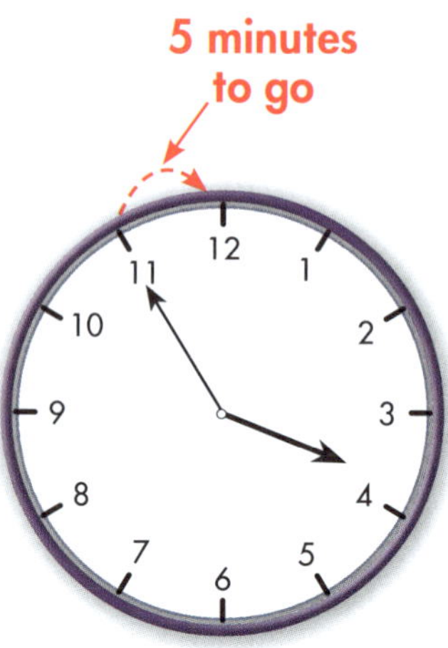

We practise

How many minutes to the next o'clock time?

11:40

20 minutes to 12

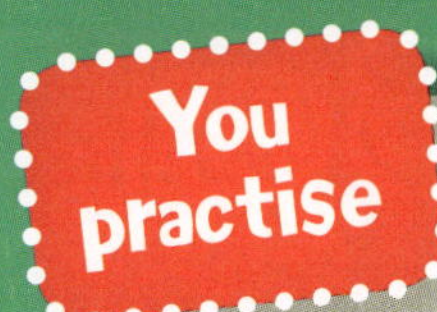

Show each time on the digital clock.

Twenty minutes past seven

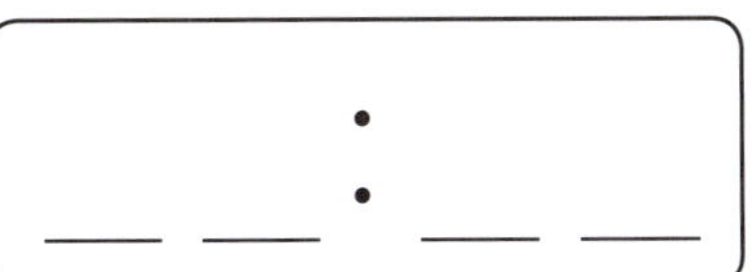

10 minutes past 6

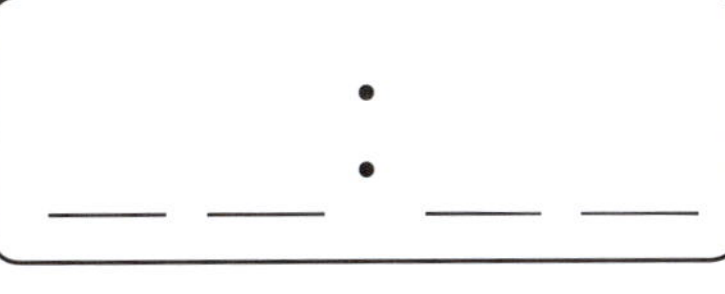

Twenty-five minutes past eleven

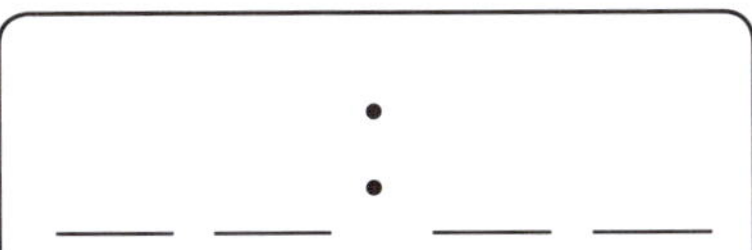

5 minutes past 3

__ __ : __ __

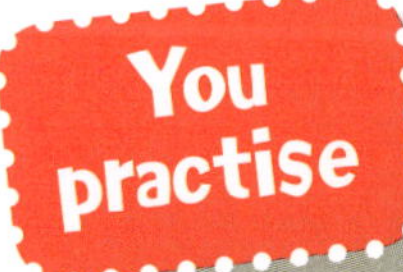

How many minutes to the next o'clock time?

3 : 40

_______ minutes to _______

5 : 35

_______ minutes to _______

6 : 50

_______ minutes to _______

2 : 55

_______ minutes to _______

7 : 40

_______ minutes to _______

6 : 45

____

ONE MINUTE INTERVALS on ANALOGUE CLOCKS

Around the edge of the clock you can see smaller marks between the five minute markers.

If you count all the spaces between these marks you will find that there are 60 spaces. This is the number of minutes in an hour. The minute hand travels all the way around the clock every hour.

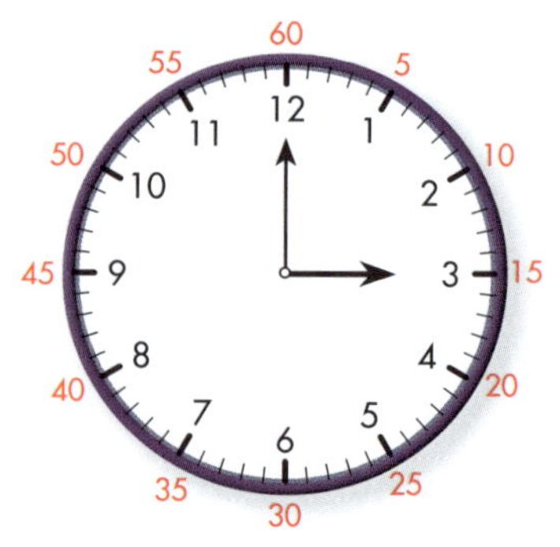

This clock shows **three minutes past seven**. Count the spaces between the 12 and where the minute hand is pointing and you will have counted the three minutes.

This clock shows a **to the hour** time.
It shows **twenty-two minutes to four**.

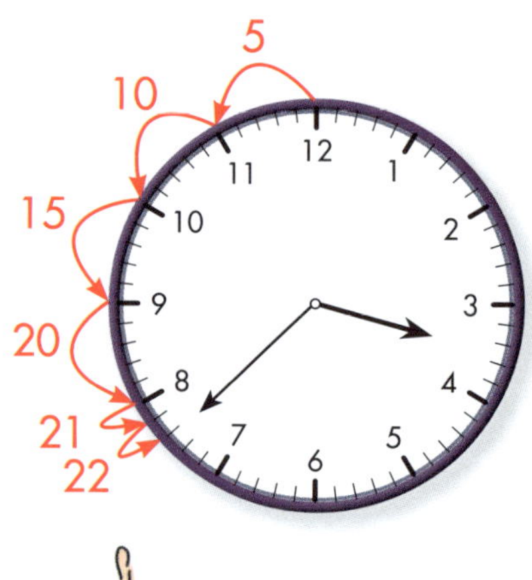

To work out how many minutes to the next hour, you can count the spaces back from the twelve. To make the counting easy, count the fives and then the extra minutes.

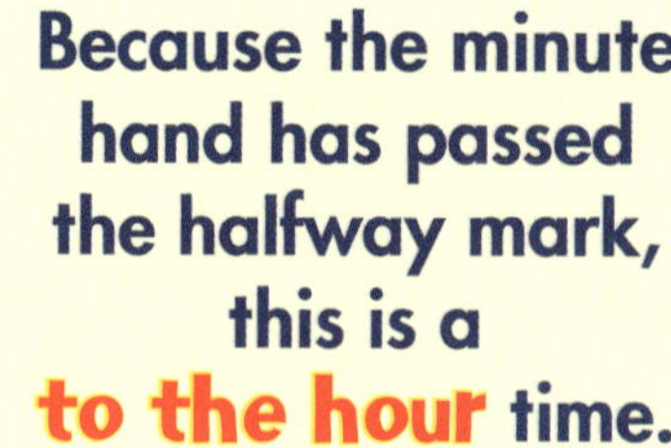

Show 17 minutes past 9 on this clock.

Show 17 minutes to 5 on this clock.

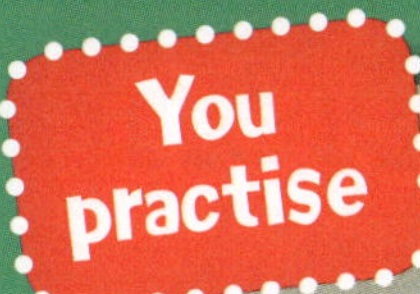

Show these 'past the hour' times on these clocks.

13 minutes past 6

28 minutes past 9

19 minutes past 1

2 minutes past 6

Think about 'close to' times like half past or quarter to.

You practise

Draw the hands on these clock faces to show the o'clock times.

13 minutes to 5

26 minutes to 3

18 minutes to 1

28 minutes to 6

7 minutes to 8

6 minutes to 11

BOB time!

ONE MINUTE INTERVALS on DIGITAL CLOCKS

Showing 'past the hour' times on the digital clock will be easy for you because you know the hour comes first followed by the number of minutes already past the hour.

26 minutes past 5 looks like this on a digital clock:

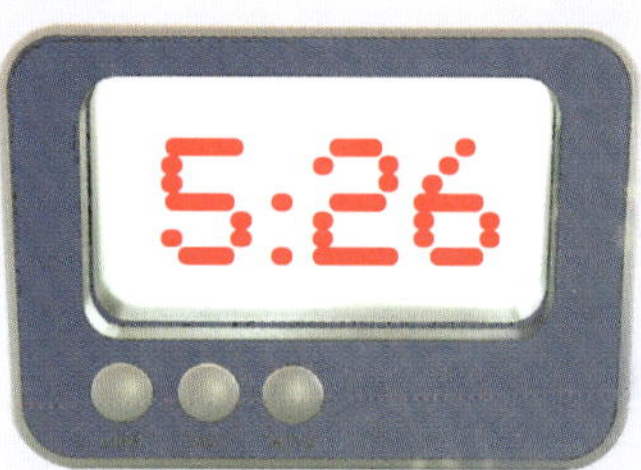

But to show **23 minutes to 7** on a digital clock, you need to stop and think. It is not 7 o'clock yet so the hour shown will be 6.

If it is 23 minutes to 7, how many minutes is that after 6 o'clock?

There are two ways of thinking about this. One way is to picture the analogue clock and count the minutes starting at 6 o'clock.

Another way is to think smart. 23 is 7 minutes away from 30 minutes, the half hour.

This helps because 30 + 7 is 37. 23 minutes to the hour is the same as saying 37 minutes past the hour.

At **23 minutes to 7**, a digital clock will look like this:

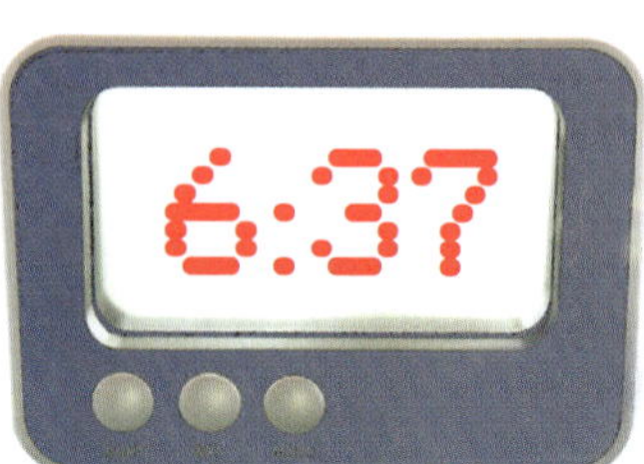

We practise

Show 28 minutes past 11 on this clock.

11:28

Show 17 minutes to 6 on this clock.

5:43

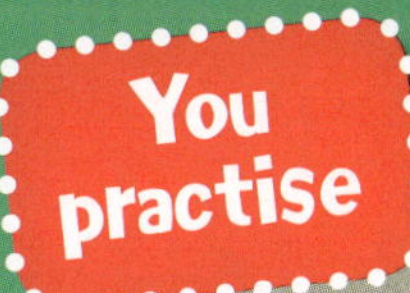

Show these 'past the hour' times on the digital clocks.

1 23 minutes past 8

__ __ : __ __

2 17 minutes past 2

__ __ : __ __

3 11 minutes past 9

__ __ : __ __

4 6 minutes past 1

__ __ : __ __

You practise

Show these 'to the hour' times on the digital clocks.

Think about 'close to' times like half past or quarter to.

5 6 minutes to 7

__ __ : __ __

6 13 minutes to 8

__ __ : __ __

7 27 minutes to 3

__ __ : __ __

8 18 minutes to 12

__ __ : __ __

9 22 minutes to 6

__ __ : __ __

10 9 minutes to 9

__ __ : __ __

BOB time!

WHAT TIME WILL IT BE?

There are some quick tricks to working out what time it will be in **half an hour** or **quarter of an hour.**

The clock below shows that in half an hour the minute hand will move halfway around the clock.

So now the time is **10 minutes to 2**.

For example, if it is **20 past 1**, as shown on the clock above, then you can use what you know to work out what time it will be in 30 minutes.

Remember to think about what the hour will be as well as thinking about the minutes.

This works for the quarters too. This clock shows how to work out what time it was 15 minutes earlier.

15 minutes is the same as quarter of an hour so a quarter turn shows the new time. So the time was **5 past 1**.

We practise

What time will this clock show in half an hour?

25 minutes to 4

What time was this clock showing quarter of an hour ago?

10 minutes to 8

You practise Write each time.

What time will this clock show in half an hour?

What time will this clock show in quarter of an hour?

What time did this clock show half an hour ago?

8:20 | __ __ : __ __

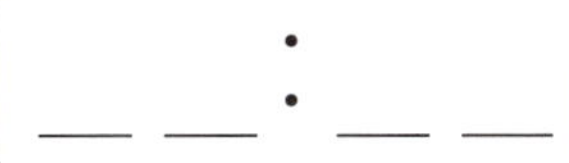

What time will this clock show in half an hour?

7:45 | __ __ : __ __

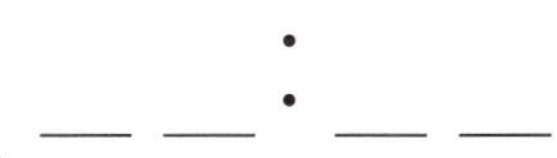

What time did this clock show half an hour ago?

What time did this clock show quarter of an hour ago?

What time did this clock show quarter of an hour ago?

8:05 | __ __ : __ __

What time will this clock show in quarter of an hour?

12:55 | __ __ : __ __

This clock shows the time that Jack gets up. He starts school one and a quarter hours later. What time is that?

Clare looks at this clock when she gets home from ballet class. If her class was for an hour and her trip home took 15 minutes, what time did she start her class?

5:50 | __ __ : __ __

MORE PROBLEM SOLVING with TIME

A Time Problem

Jack said he was in training for the athletics carnival. He said that he will train every month from the first month of autumn until the carnival at the end of July. How many months will he train for?

The first month of autumn is March, so making a quick list and counting will answer the problem.
March, April, May, June, July = 5 months
Jake will train for 5 months.

Notice that the important information is highlighted in blue and what has to be found out is highlighted in pink.

Remember to write the answer as a sentence.

We practise

Highlight the important information and what you have to find out in this problem and then find the solution.

Clare has a dentist appointment in October. It is not at the weekend and it is not in the first or the last week of the month. It is not the first day of the school week. It is a single digit date. What day and date is Clare going to the dentist?

OCTOBER 2013						
Sunday	Monday	Tuesday	Wednesday	Thursday	Friday	Saturday
	1	2	3	4	5	6
7	8	9	10	11	12	13
14	15	16	17	18	19	20
21	22	23	24	25	26	27
28	29	30	31			

Answer: Clare is going to the dentist on Tuesday the 9th of October.

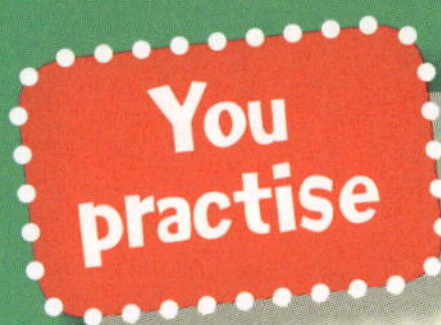

Highlight the important information and solve these problems.

1 Clare said her favourite month is the middle month in the coldest season. What is Clare's favourite month? Clare's favourite month is ________________.

2 Jake went away during October 2012. He was gone from early on the first Monday of the month until late on the second Friday. How many days was Jake away for? Jake was away for __________ days.

3 Mum said to set the clock for 10 minutes past 7 but Clare set it for 10 to 7. What time did her clock show? __ __ : __ __

4 The TV program begins at 6:45 and lasts for half an hour. What time will the clock show at the end of the program?

5 Jake was half an hour late for his trumpet lesson. He was due at 5:45. What time did Jake arrive at the lesson? __ __ : __ __

6 Clare had to get up at 7:15. She set her alarm half an hour early to make sure she was wide awake at 7:15. What time did her clock show when the alarm went off? Clare's alarm went off at __________.

7 It took Jake 45 minutes to do his homework. If he started at 6:15, what time did he finish? Jake finished at __________.

8 Clare started cooking pizza at 12:20. It took her an hour and fifteen minutes to make. What time was the pizza ready? The pizza was ready at __________.

9 The first month of the school year is February and the last month of the school year is December. What is the middle month of the school year? The middle month of the school year is ________________.

10 The movie starts at 6:30 and goes for one and a half hours. What time does the movie finish? The movie finishes at __________.

BOB time!

TEST 1

What o'clock time is this clock face showing?

_______ o'clock

What time does this clock face show?

_______ o'clock

Show 7 o'clock on this digital clock.

__ __ : __ __

Write the digital time for each event in the correct order and then draw a line to match each event with the digital time.

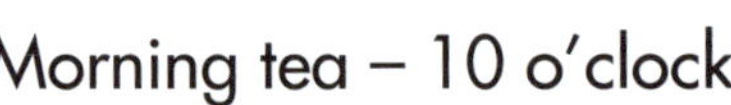

Morning tea – 10 o'clock

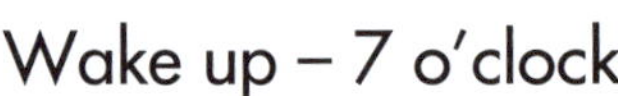

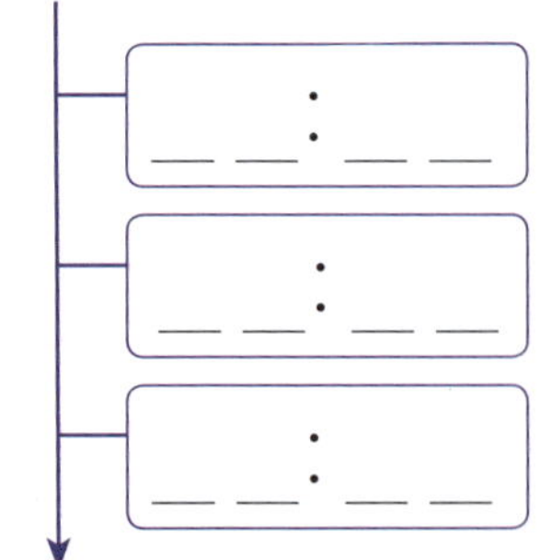

Draw the hands to show half past four on this clock face.

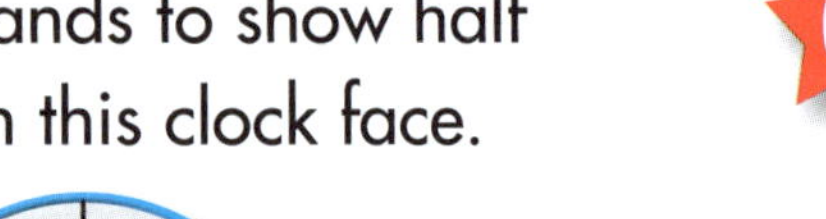

Write the analogue clock time on the digital clock.

Draw the hands to show quarter past seven on this clock face.

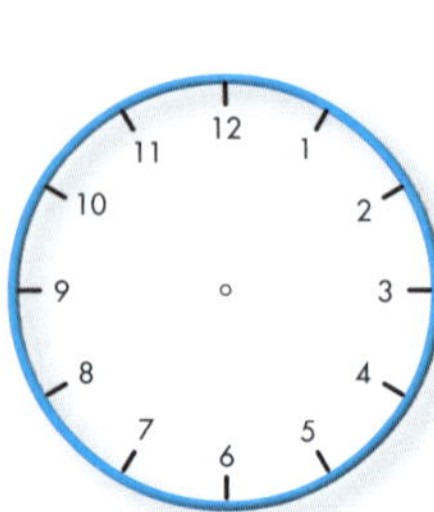

Show quarter past eight on this digital clock.

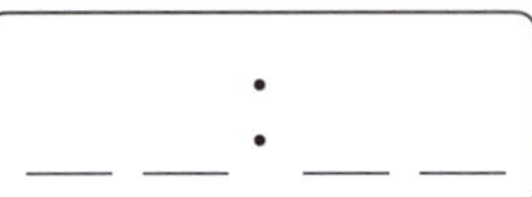

Write the missing days in this list:

Saturday, ____________, ____________, Tuesday

Clare said she went to the movies yesterday and that tomorrow, which is Tuesday, she is going to her friend's to play. What day is it today?

____________________.

TEST 2

Write the missing months in this list:

November, ____________, ____________, February

List the winter months: ____________, ____________, ____________.

What times do these clocks show?

________ minutes past ________

4

7:20

________ minutes past ________

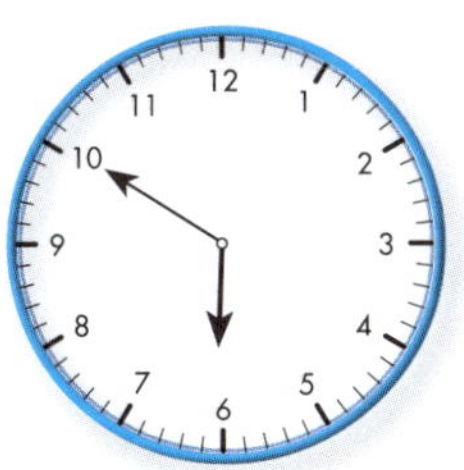

________ minutes to ________

10:40

________ minutes to ________

________ minutes past ________

1:44

________ minutes to ________

How many minutes in three quarters of an hour? ____________ minutes

Jack is going on holiday three weeks from today. On the fourth day on holiday he is visiting his Nan and staying at her house overnight.
If today is Tuesday, what day of the week will it be when he wakes up at his Nan's in the morning?

____________________.

Look back through the book for help if you need to.

ANSWERS

Unit 1

1

2
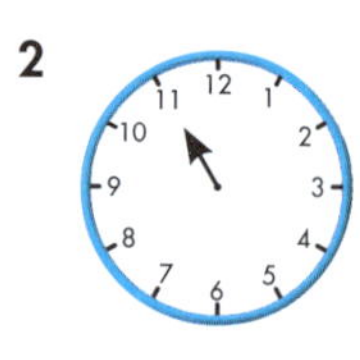

3

4
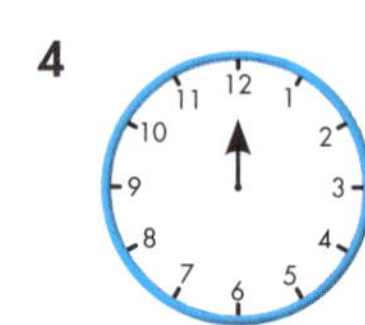

5 5 o'clock
6 8 o'clock
7 4 o'clock
8 7 o'clock
9 6 o'clock
10 10 o'clock

Unit 2

1 6 o'clock
2 10 o'clock
3 9 o'clock
4 1 o'clock

5
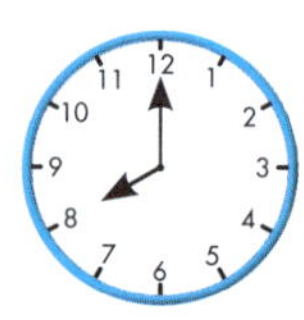

6

7

8

9

10

Unit 3

1	5:00	
2	9:00	
3	11:00	
4	3:00	
5	2:00	two o'clock
6	7:00	seven o'clock
7	10:00	ten o'clock
8	1:00	one o'clock
9	8:00	eight o'clock
10	12:00	twelve o'clock

Unit 4

Bedtime – 9 o'clock
Breakfast – 8 o'clock
Lunch time – 12 o'clock
Dinner time – 7 o'clock
Get out of bed – 7 o'clock
Watch TV – 8 o'clock
Karate – 5 o'clock
Haircut – 10 o'clock
Meet friend for afternoon walk – 2 o'clock
Afternoon snack with Mum – 4 o'clock

7:00
8:00
10:00
12:00
2:00
4:00
5:00
7:00
8:00
9:00

Unit 5

1 half past two
2 half past ten
3 half past four
4 half past seven

5
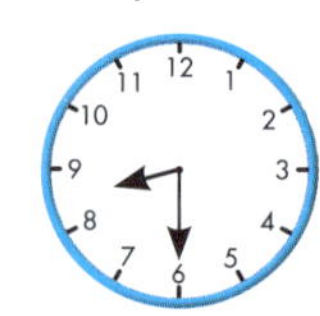

6
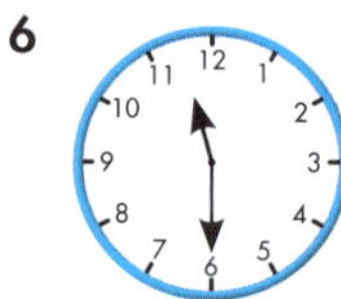

7
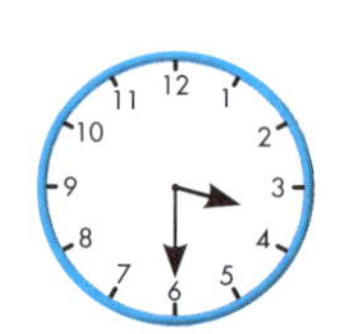

8
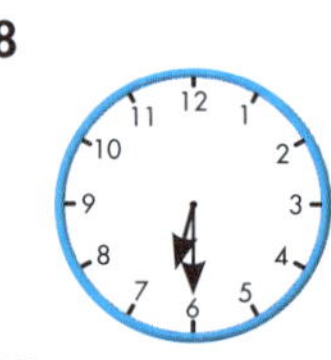

9
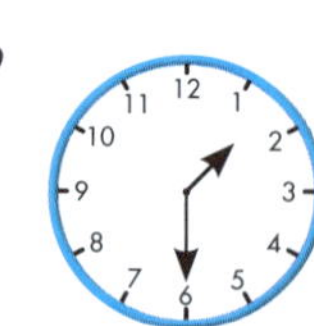

10

Unit 6

1 half past nine
2 half past seven
3 half past four
4 half past eleven

5	3:30
6	8:30
7	11:30
8	2:30
9	10:30
10	12:30

ANSWERS

Unit 7

1 Friday
2 Wednesday
3 Sunday
4 Thursday
5 Saturday and Sunday
6 Sunday
7 Friday
8 Saturday
9 Wednesday
10 Tuesday

Unit 8

1 quarter past two
2 quarter past six
3 quarter past ten
4 quarter past seven

5 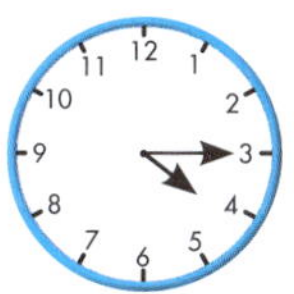

6 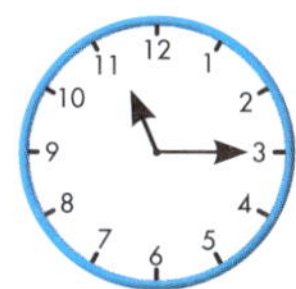

7 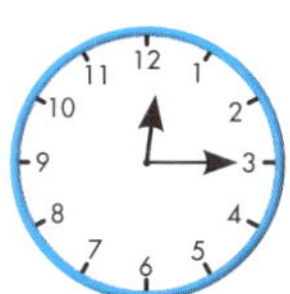

8 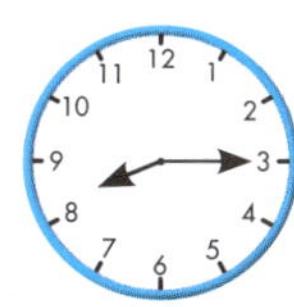

9 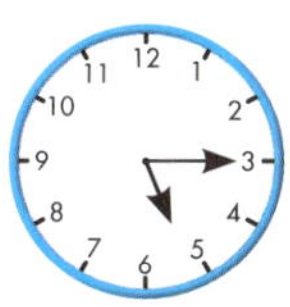

10 

Unit 9

1 quarter past one
2 quarter past four
3 quarter past six
4 quarter past five
5 9:15
6 2:15
7 7:15
8 8:15
9 4:15
10 12:15

Unit 10

1 6:15
2 Saturday
3 Saturday
4 Wednesday
5 two o'clock or 2:00
6 3:30

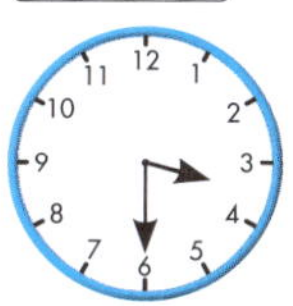

7 6:00 or six o'clock
8 5:15

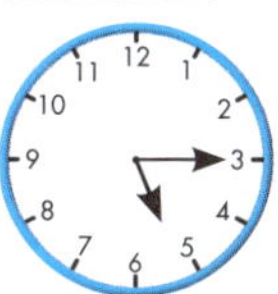

Unit 11

1 November
2 July
3 March
4 January
5 January
6 June
7 winter
8 summer
9 winter
10 summer

Unit 12

1 Friday, 27th December
2 18th December
3 Tuesday
4 14th December
5 January 2014
6 3 times
7 2000
8 5 Sundays
9 23rd December
10 Adding each pair of numbers gives the same total.

ANSWERS

Unit 13

1 quarter to 10
2 quarter to 4
3 quarter to 8
4 quarter to 11

5 
6 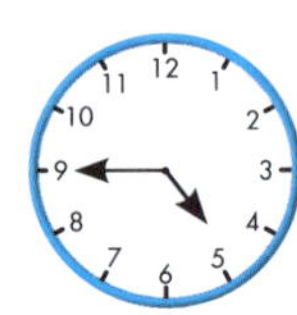
7 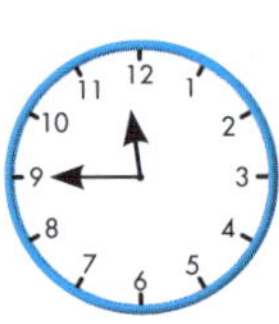
8 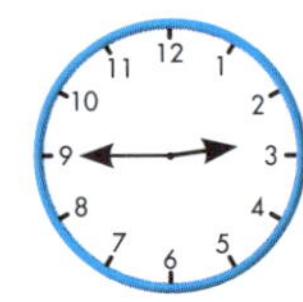
9 
10 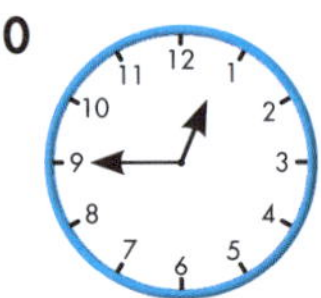

Unit 14

1 quarter to 2
2 quarter to 4
3 quarter to 11
4 quarter to 1
5 7:45
6 7:45
7 11:45
8 12:45

9 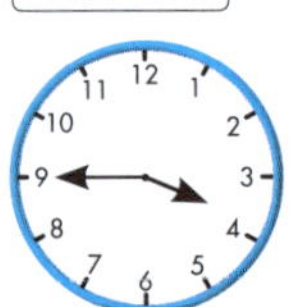
10 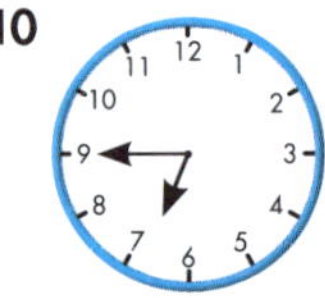

Unit 15

1 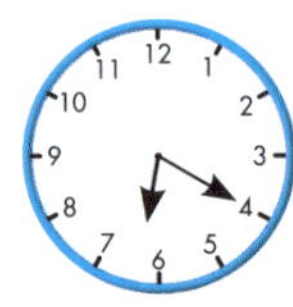
2 
3 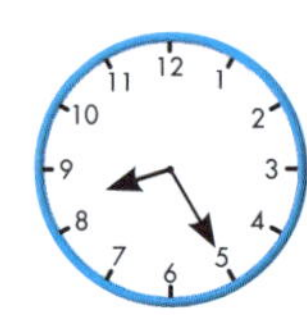
4 
5 
6 
7 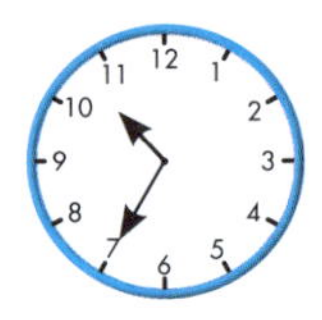
8 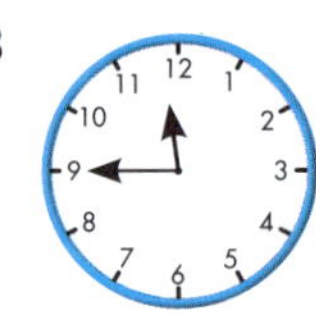
9 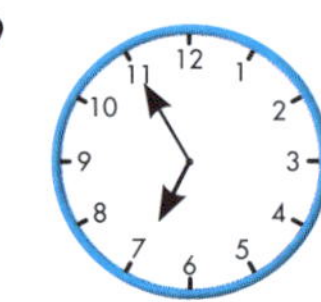
10 

Unit 16

1 7:20
2 6:10
3 11:25
4 3:05
5 20 minutes to 4
6 25 minutes to 6
7 10 minutes to 7
8 5 minutes to 3
9 20 minutes to 8
10 quarter to 7

Unit 17

1 
2 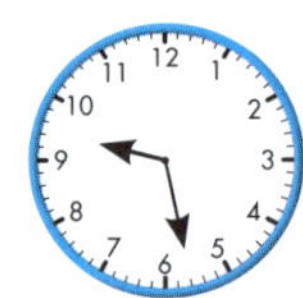
3 
4 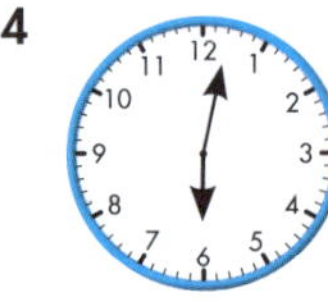
5 
6 
7 
8 
9 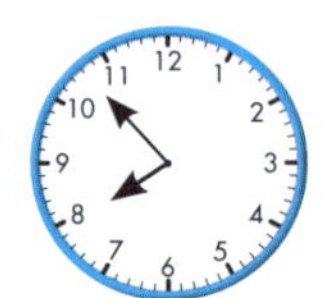
10 

ANSWERS

Unit 18

1. 8:23
2. 2:17
3. 9:11
4. 1:06
5. 6:54
6. 7:47
7. 2:33
8. 11:42
9. 5:38
10. 8:51

Unit 19

1. quarter to 6
2. 5 minutes past 3
3. 7:50
4. 8:15
5. 10 minutes past 5
6. 5 minutes to 4
7. 7:50
8. 1:10
9. quarter to 9
10. 4:35

Unit 20

1. July
2. 12 days
3. 6:50
4. 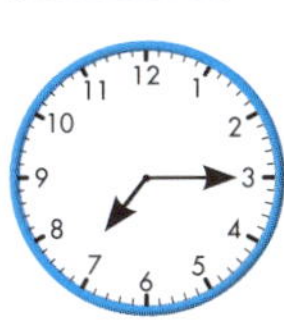
5. 6:15
6. 6:45
7. 7:00
8. 1:35
9. July
10. 8:00

Test 1

1. 4 o'clock
2. 5 o'clock
3. 7:00
4. Swimming – 3 o'clock
   Morning tea – 10 o'clock
   Wake up – 7 o'clock

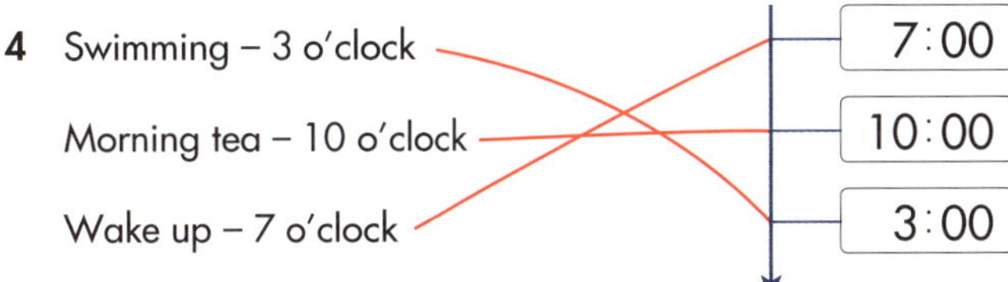

5.
6. 3:30
7.
8. 8:15
9. Sunday, Monday
10. Monday

Test 2

1. December, January
2. June, July, August
3. 10 minutes past 2
4. 20 minutes past 7
5. 10 minutes to 6
6. 20 minutes to 11
7. 10 minutes past 4
8. 16 minutes to 2
9. 45 minutes
10. Saturday

Back to Basics Time Years 2–3

Reprinted 2015, 2018, 2022

ISBN: 978 1 74215 936 2

Published by Pascal Press
PO Box 250
Glebe NSW 2037
www.pascalpress.com.au
contact@pascalpress.com.au

Author: Ann Baker
Publisher: Lynn Dickinson
Editor: Tim Learner
Proofreader: Ruth Schultz
Design and illustration: Janice Bowles
Cover design: Deb Snibson, MAPG
Printed by Wai Man Book Binding (China) Ltd.